Scripture Memory made easy

Mark Water

HENDRICKSON
PUBLISHERS

Scripture Memory Made Easy
Hendrickson Publishers, Inc.
P.O. Box 3473
Peabody, Massachusetts 01961-3473

ISBN 1-56563-106-4

Designed and produced
by Tony Cantale Graphics

First printing — July 1999
Reprinted 2001
Manufactured in China

Photography supplied by Foxx
Photos, Goodshoot, Digital Vision,
Photo Alto and Tony Cantale

Illustrations by
Tony Cantale Graphics

Contents

Special pull-out chart

Plan for learning one hundred Bible verses in fifty-two weeks

Why bother learning Bible verses?

Memorizing Bible verses helps you:
- to understand God's Word
- to pray
- to meditate on God's Word
- to share Jesus with others
- to counter Satan's attacks

Remember it is God's Word

"For the word of God is living and active. Sharper than any double-edged sword, it penetrates even to dividing soul and spirit, joints and marrow; it judges the thoughts and attitudes of the heart."
Hebrews 4:12

Remember it is God's inspired Word

"But as for you, continue in what you have learned and have become convinced of, because you know those from whom you learned it, and how from infancy you have known the holy Scriptures, which are able to make you wise for salvation through faith in Christ Jesus. All Scripture is God-breathed and is useful for teaching, rebuking, correcting and training in righteousness, so that the man of God may be thoroughly equipped for every good work." *2 Timothy 3:14-17*

Motivation for memorizing scripture

You need to be motivated:
- to get you started
- so you won't give up

Don't worry if you think:

- **"My memory is terrible"** – this book will help you train your memory to remember Bible verses.
- **"I've tried it before"** – here is a simple way to help you, no matter how many times you may have tried to do this before.
- **"I don't know how to do this"** – this book gives you a step by step approach and assumes that you know nothing about memorizing Scripture.
- **"I've always wanted to memorize Scripture but I'm worried that I'll just give up"** – this book will keep on showing you how you can persevere in memorizing Scripture.

Motivation

What we enjoy doing most, we do best.

If you think of learning Bible verses merely as a laborious chore, you will find it much more difficult unless you realize that it will:
- help you become a stronger Christian
- help you to be more effective for Jesus.

Memorizing Scripture *is* hard work. It's no good starting to memorize Scripture thinking that it will be a breeze.

Perseverence is needed. But it is a joy and a privilege to draw closer to God in this way.

> "The law of the LORD is perfect, reviving the soul.
> The statutes of the LORD are trustworthy, making wise the simple.
> The precepts of the LORD are right, giving joy to the heart.
> The commands of the LORD are radiant, giving light to the eyes."
>
> *Psalm 19:7-8*

Flawless . . . like pure gold

Memorizing Scripture is unlike memorizing anything else. Some of the techniques may be used when memorizing Shakespeare or reviewing for an exam. But the *purpose* is different. The *material* is unique.

> "And the WORDS of the Lord are flawless, like silver refined in a furnace of clay, purified seven times." *Psalm 12:6*

> "Because I love your commands more than gold, more than pure gold." *Psalm 119:127*

Build yourself up so you can help others

> "Let the word of Christ
> dwell in you richly
> as you teach
> and admonish one another with all wisdom,
> and as you sing psalms, hymns and spiritual songs
> with gratitude in your hearts to God."
> *Colossians 3:16*

What to do before you start

1. Pray
Ask God to help you as you prepare to undertake this task.

Ask God for his help as you memorize Scripture.

> "[God] answered their prayers, because they trusted in him."
> *1 Chronicles 5:20*

2. Be positive
You *can* memorize Scripture. Have a positive attitude as you start.

3. Which Bible should I use?
Use an accurate translation. Memorize all your verses in the same translation.

Use your current or favorite Bible as the basis for memorizing Scripture, but be certain that the translation is accurate. You probably should not use a paraphrase in scriptural memorization.

4. When should I memorize Scripture?
There are no rules here. Whenever is best for you is the best time. Some people make it part of the time while they are praying and reading their Bible. Some find first thing in the morning and last thing at night are good times for this.

5. Using memory cards
Obtain 100 white 3 x 5 index cards. Blank business cards sold by stationers are also ideal. You can carry them around with you in a little holder or credit card wallet.

Write one Bible verse on each card as you prepare to memorize it.

You may prefer to access the Bible verse on your computer and print it out in a small font on a stiff piece of paper which you can then cut up.

Then you are ready to carry around the verses with you at all times.

The Sadducees

The Sadducees in Jesus' day probably knew the Scriptures (our Old Testament) better than nearly all Christians today. But Jesus told them: "'You are in error because you do not know the Scriptures or the power of God'" *Matthew 22:29.* They knew the words of the Scripture, but in their hearts they did not know its meaning or its power.

As you memorize Scripture make sure that you don't think this will by itself make you a better Christian. Unless the verses sink into your soul, there will be little change in your life.

6. Remember your goal

Your goal in memorizing Scripture is to become more and more like Jesus. Keep this goal in mind for it is quite possible to memorize dozens of Bible verses and yet receive little or no spiritual benefit.

Do what the Word says

"Do not merely listen to the word, and so deceive yourselves. Do what it says. Anyone who listens to the word but does not do what it says is like a man who looks at his face in a mirror and, after looking at himself, goes away and immediately forgets what he looks like." *James 1:22-24*

Learning your first Bible verse

At last!
Now it is time to learn your first Bible verse. It's written out on this page as if it were on the card that you are going to write it on.

Learning the verse
Determine whether the verse divides into sections. This first verse has three sections.

SIX KEYS   1/1/1
Loved by Jesus

"As the Father has loved me, so have I loved you. Now remain in my love."
John 15:9

- Start with the first phrase: As the Father has loved me. Learn that.
- Then memorize the second phrase: so have I loved you.
- Now see if you can say the first two phrases without looking at them.
- When you can, memorize the third phrase: Now remain in my love.
- Now try the whole verse. Keep on doing this until you're certain that you know the verse forward and backward!

Learning the Bible reference
If you are familiar with Bible references, you know that John 15:9 stands for where the verse comes in the Bible. John is for John's Gospel, 15 is for chapter 15, and 9 is for verse 9.

You should now memorize the reference. Then say the verse and its reference. Every time you learn a new Bible verse memorize its reference as well.

The Bible memory card

You will see five things on this card.

1. The top left hand corner has the words Six keys. This is the theme for the first six Bible verses you are going to learn. From the pull down chart at the end of the book you will see the next themes are: God's plan of salvation and Six "I am's" of Jesus.

2. The second line on the top left hand corner of the card says Loved by Jesus. This is the topic the verse deals with. This sub-heading helps you to see the point of the verse you are memorizing. These topic headings will also help you to remember all the different verses you have memorized.

3. The top right hand corner has 1/1/1. The first 1 stands for the year. The first year's worth of memory verses is year one. This 1 will only become 2 after you have learned 100 verses.

The second 1 refers to the week of the year you are in. As this is the first week you are learning a Bible verse it is week 1. This means that you do not have to wait for January until you start. Week 1 is the week you start the course and that can be at any time in the year.

The third 1 indicates it is the first verse you have learned this week. These numbers help you to keep the cards in the order that you are learning the verses and put them back into that order should you drop them all!

4. The Bible verse itself is written out in the center of the card.

5. The Bible reference follows the Bible verse.

A plan for each week

Monday to Sunday

Monday	Learn the first verse for the week. There are only two verses to learn each week. That might seem rather slow to start with. But under this plan you end up memorizing one hundred verses each year. If you want to learn more than two verses a week you may do so, of course. But bear in mind is that some people find they give up memorizing verses altogether because it becomes too much for them.
Tuesday	Review your verses. This is explained on pages 16-17 under the topic *How do I review verses?*
Wednesday	Learn the second verse for the week. For each verse that you learn, write out the Bible verse on a card in the way that was explained in the previous two pages. Remember there are five things to place on each card. This book lists the one hundred verses for the first year, so all you have to do is to copy them.
Thursday	Review the two verses you have learned for this week.
Friday	Review your verses. This is explained on pages 16-17 under the topic *How do I review verses?*
Saturday	Review this week's verses again.
Sunday	Day off.

Strive for 100% accuracy

Settle for nothing less than 100% accuracy as you learn each verse. If you learn verses in even a slightly inaccurate way, you'll find it difficult in the future when you try to remember them.

I'm a slow learner

Don't worry if you do not have a photographic memory! The longer a verse takes to remember, the better because you will end up knowing it more thoroughly.

How to learn a verse

1. Read the whole verse. If possible, read it out aloud.
2. Pray to understand its meaning for you.
3. Break the verse into small parts. The punctuation in the verse often does this for you.
4. Then state the name of the topic, the first phrase of the Bible verse, and the Bible reference.
5. Add in the second phrase, and repeat the name of the topic, the first two phrases of the Bible verse and the Bible reference.
6. Keep adding in phrases until you have completed the verse.
7. Say by heart just the Bible verse three times.
8. Say by heart the topic, the Bible verse and the Bible reference.

Think about it from God's viewpoint

Did you know that God *wants* you to memorize his Word?

"These commandments that I give you today are to be upon your hearts." *Deuteronomy 6:6*

Your first week of memory verses

Here is your first week of verses.

Use *How to learn a verse* from page 13 when you learn your verses.

As this is your first week, and you have no verses to review, use your review days to check that these two verses are really part of your life. See what each verse means, and what it means for you. Think about whether the verses have changed your thinking, attitudes, or behavior in any way.

SIX KEYS	1/1/1
Loved by Jesus	

"As the Father has loved me, so have I loved you. Now remain in my love."
John 15:9

SIX KEYS	1/1/2
Loved by the Father	

"For God so loved the world that he gave his one and only Son, that whoever believes in him shall not perish but have eternal life."
John 3:16

More than merely memorizing words

Memorizing Scripture is more than memorizing words. While much time is spent on the mechanics of actually getting the verses into your brain, don't forget that this is just a small part of the course.

The lost art of meditating on Bible verses

If you have learned a Bible verse by heart, you can now meditate on it. You don't have to read it from your Bible. Since it is in your head, you can meditate on it wherever you are.

"But his delight is in the law of the LORD,
and on his law he meditates day and night."
Psalm 1:2

Meditating on the truths contained in Bible verses is not like day dreaming or any other kind of meditation. The Psalmist is specific – he says that he meditates on God's law.

How does this apply to me?

There is little point in remembering dozens of Bible verses and never asking yourself the question: How can this verse help me in my Christian life? One good way to do this is to see what there is in each verse that you can thank God for and then pray to God and thank him for that. Look for challenges, commands, and wonderful things about God himself in the verses you learn.

A habit for life

You are on the brink of acquiring a habit of learning Scripture. This could transform your Christian life. So be patient. Take the course seriously. And persevere.

"How do I review verses?"

Learning and forgetting
Most people find that by tomorrow they have forgotten the verse they learned today. They simply learn and forget.

Learning and remembering
The way to learn and remember is to review what you have learned. This means repeating today what you learned yesterday. It means repeating, repeating, repeating, day after day, after day, after day.

Review days: Tuesdays and Fridays

Here is a review plan. It is as important as the plan for memorizing verses.

On page 12, *A plan for each week*, you will see that Tuesdays and Fridays are set aside for reviewing. These are the days that you review the Bible verses which you have previously memorized.

Review plan for the year

Your second week's verses

Here are the two verses for your second week

You'll see that they continue the theme of love. Last week you memorized about how you are loved by Jesus and loved by God the Father. The first verse for this week focuses on how this love of God comes to us through the Holy Spirit. The second verse for this week centers on how Jesus loved us so much that he died for us.

As you progress with this course, look at each verse and before you memorize it. Pray about what it is saying to you personally.

SIX KEYS	1/2/1

Loved through the Spirit

And hope does not disappoint us, because God has poured out his love into our hearts by the Holy Spirit, whom he has given us.
Romans 5:5

SIX KEYS	1/2/2

No greater love

"Greater love has no one than this, that he lay down his life for his friends."
John 15:13

Plan for your second week of Scripture memory

Monday	Learn Romans 5:5.
Tuesday	Review your verses from week 1. Take the card 1/1/1 and look at the topic in the right hand corner: Loved by Jesus. Now say the verse and its reference. Check and double check that you are 100% accurate. Do the same with card 1/1/2. Now say the topics, Bible verse, and reference for both days.
Wednesday	Learn John 15:13.
Thursday	Review the two verses you have learned for this week.
Friday	Review your verses from week 1, as you did on Tuesday.
Saturday	Review this week's verses again.
Sunday	Day off.

Write out your verses

One good way to check that you have managed to remember your verses with complete accuracy is to write them out. Write out the two Bible verses and their Bible references for the first week and check them carefully to see that they are perfect, word for word.

How to "picture" your verses

Make learning fun

Some people just love memorizing and need no incentives or helps at all. But most people think negatively about learning in this manner.

Make sure that however you go about learning these Bible verses that you follow a way that you enjoy and, if possible, find full of fun.

Hearing and "seeing"

Communications experts tell us that our sight gives us 83% of our total sensory input, our hearing gives us 11%, our sense of smell gives us 4%, and our sense of taste 2%. Obviously, our sight and hearing are our most important senses. The table below shows how much of their input we remember.

	After 3 hours	After 3 days
Hearing only	70%	10%
Sight only	72%	20%
Hearing and sight	85%	65%

This shows that the spoken word is more easily remembered if the hearer is able to visualize it and "see" what is being said.

Preach the words

Imagine that you are in the pulpit in the biggest church in the world. You are about to tell the packed church about these wonderful words from Scripture. You announce your text: "And hope does not disappoint us, because God has poured out his love into our hearts by the Holy Spirit, whom he has given us."

Say them slowly

Say the words out aloud.

From your pulpit say the words in a way that bring out their meaning.

Emphasize the words which you think are the key words. Introduce pauses, to allow your congregation to take in the meaning of the verse, phrase by phrase.

Romans 5:5

Your first verse for week 2 might be said in the following way.

"And hope
does not disappoint us,
because God has poured out
his love
into our hearts
by the Holy Spirit,
whom he has given us."

Use your imagination

Think of yourself reading this letter for the first time to the early Christians in Rome, huddled together in a Christian's home, listening eagerly to every word from the letter of the famous theologian and missionary, Paul: "And hope does not disappoint us, because God has poured out his love into our hearts by the Holy Spirit, whom he has given us."

Your third week's verses

Here are your verses for your third week. Observe what they are about before you learn them.

SIX KEYS	1/3/1
God is love	
And so we know and rely on the love God has for us. God is love. Whoever lives in love lives in God, and God in him. 1 John 4:16	

SIX KEYS	1/3/2
No separation from love	
. . . neither height nor depth, nor anything else in all creation, will be able to separate us from the love of God that is in Christ Jesus our Lord. Romans 8:39	

Monday to Sunday

Monday	Learn 1 John 4:16.
Tuesday	The verses to review this week are the verses from weeks 1 and 2. On pages 16–17, under the table *Review plan for the year*, you will see which verses you have to review each week.
Wednesday	Learn Romans 8:39.
Thursday	Review the two verses you have learned for this week.
Friday	Repeat what you did on Tuesday.
Saturday	Review this week's two verses again.
Sunday	Day off.

Memory aid

Each theme has been given a memory aid, and they are noted on the pull out section at the end of the book. Unsurprisingly, the memory aid for the first three weeks of verses is: KEY.

Themes

The one hundred verses to be learned have been divided into twelve themes:

1 Six keys to the Christian life

2 God's plan of salvation

3 Jesus' six "I am's"

4 The Holy Spirit at work

5 Bible promises

6 Jesus and his cross

7 How can I be sure that I am a Christian?

8 How can I grow as a Christian?

9 Witnessing for Jesus

10 Words of comfort

11 Psalm 23

12 1 Corinthians 13

Handy hints about your memory

Do you have a bad memory?

Most of us think that we do have a bad memory. We often find it hard to remember anything longer than a short sentence.

But this is not because we have a bad memory. It is because we have an untrained memory. This course will help train your memory.

Review

As a piano teacher says, "Practice, practice, practice," so this Scripture memory course says, "Review, review, review."

One of the keys to successful memory work is reviewing what you have learned. Don't skip the reviewing this course gives you. It is the most permanent way of learning. Look forward to reviewing – it is the key to successfully remembering Scripture.

If you forget a word

When you forget a word in a Bible verse, repeat the phrase that contains the word three times. Then say the whole verse three times.

Do you have a patient friend?

If so, say your verses to him or her.

Listen to the verse

Record the verse on a cassette. Start with the topic, then the verse and its reference.

You could do this for all one hundred verses. How surprised people would be if they knew what you were listening to on your Walkman!

"Practice makes perfect"

"Practice makes perfect" is a phrase used by memory teaching experts. All they are saying is: put into practice what you have learned. For a Christian who is learning Bible verses, there could be no better advice.

As Christians, we know that we are meant to live out in our lives what we discover in the Bible. As we do this, it also helps us remember particular Bible verses.

Reading, hearing, speaking

When you link reading, hearing, and speaking you are much more likely to remember what you learn. When you make use of your Bible knowledge, you are reinforcing the learning process.

- So read the verses you are learning.
- Listen to the verses you are learning by saying them aloud or listening to a cassette.
- "Speak" the Bible verses as you put into practice the verses you are learning, by talking about them with others, or meditating on them in your heart.

Weeks 4–6: God's plan of salvation

GOD'S PLAN OF SALVATION
1/4/1
All are lost

We all, like sheep, have gone astray, each of us has turned to his own way; and the LORD has laid on him the iniquity of us all.
Isaiah 53:6

GOD'S PLAN OF SALVATION
1/4/2
All have sinned

. . . for all have sinned and fall short of the glory of God.
Romans 3:23

GOD'S PLAN OF SALVATION
1/5/1
Sin ends in death

For the wages of sin is death, but the gift of God is eternal life in Christ Jesus our Lord.
Romans 6:23

GOD'S PLAN OF SALVATION
1/5/2
Jesus died to bring you to God

For Christ died for sins once for all, the righteous for the unrighteous, to bring you to God. He was put to death in the body but made alive by the Spirit.
1 Peter 3:18

GOD'S PLAN OF SALVATION
1/6/1
Jesus took your sins

He himself bore our sins in his body on the tree, so that we might die to sins and live for righteousness; by his wounds you have been healed.
1 Peter 2:24

GOD'S PLAN OF SALVATION
1/6/2
Come in, Lord Jesus

"Here I am! I stand at the door and knock. If anyone hears my voice and opens the door, I will come in and eat with him, and he with me."
Revelation 3:20

There are six verses in this second theme of *God's plan of salvation*. They are set out for you to learn over the next three weeks.

The bridge illustration

These verses are often linked to the bridge illustration as a way of helping someone to see what Jesus did on the cross.

People

On the left hand side of the bridge are people. They depict the plight that everyone is in.

The first three verses of *God's plan of salvation* spell out the spiritual condition of humankind: all have sinned, all are lost, and sin ends in death.

The cross

The central part of the bridge shows the cross of Jesus. The purpose of Jesus' death is stated in the next two verses: Jesus died to bring you to God, and Jesus died for your sins.

God

On the right hand side of the illustration is God. We come to God by making the last verse we are learning in this theme into a prayer. We ask the Lord Jesus to come into our lives in response to his knocking on the door of our lives.

Weeks 7–9: Six "I am's" of Jesus

SIX "I AM'S" OF JESUS 1/7/1	SIX "I AM'S" OF JESUS 1/7/2	SIX "I AM'S" OF JESUS 1/8/1
Bread	Light	Gate
Then Jesus declared, "I am the bread of life. He who comes to me will never go hungry, and he who believes in me will never be thirsty." John 6:35	When Jesus spoke again to the people he said, "I am the light of the world. Whoever follows me will never walk in darkness, but will have the light of life." John 8:12	"I am the gate; whoever enters through me will be saved. He will come in and go out, and find pasture." John 10:9

SIX "I AM'S" OF JESUS 1/8/2	SIX "I AM'S" OF JESUS 1/9/1	SIX "I AM'S" OF JESUS 1/9/2
Good Shepherd	Resurrection and life	Way, Truth, Life
"I am the good shepherd. The good shepherd lays down his life for the sheep." John 10:11	Jesus said to her, "I am the resurrection and the life. He who believes in me will live, even though he dies." John 11:25	Jesus answered, "I am the way and the truth and the life. No one comes to the Father except through me." John 14:6

John's Gospel
One of the most helpful ways to recall who Jesus is, is to mull over what he said about himself. In John's Gospel he explains who he is by using the words, "I am."

More and more verses
By the end of this theme, you will have learned eighteen verses. You may be wondering how you are going to remember them all, especially as you are adding to them at the rate of two a week.

Pull-out chart

The pull-out chart at the end of this book has a number of lists.

1. It lists the fifty-two weeks of the year.
2. It lists the Bible references of the one hundred Bible verses
3. It lists the topic for each of the Bible verses
4. It lists the twelve themes for the whole year

Rocket

On the right hand side is a rocket. This links all the themes as an aid to your memory. It uses an abbreviation or symbol for each theme, and depicts this inside a room in the space ship. The idea is to make it easy to remember that your verses start with a key, then follow a plan. The six "I am's" are depicted by a giant placard with the words "I am" on it.

"What do I do when I want to give up?"

This is quite normal

Most people find that they go through a time, or many times, when they feel like giving up learning Bible verses.

A spiritual activity

Memorizing Scripture, if engaged in properly, launches you into a spiritual battle. Satan does not want you to stick with it to the end. He will stop at nothing to keep you from growing closer and closer to Jesus.

Satan will not be happy that you are learning Bible verses.

> "Be self-controlled and alert. Your enemy the devil prowls around like a roaring lion looking for someone to devour." *1 Peter 5:8*

So what are we to do? How do we respond? Peter continues:

> "Resist him, standing firm in the faith, because you know that your brothers throughout the world are undergoing the same kind of sufferings." *1 Peter 5:9*

Learning difficulties

If one particular verse seems difficult to learn, try this idea.

Go back to reading the verse from your card instead of attempting to recite it from memory.

Read it aloud "word by word" and "syllable by syllable." Use 1 Peter 3:18: "For Christ died for sins once for all, the righteous for the unrighteous, to bring you to God. He was put to death in the body but made alive by the Spirit." Read it slowly like this:

> *For – Christ – died – for – sins – once – for – all, – the – right-eous – for – the – un-right-eous, – to – bring – you – to – God. – He – was – put – to – death – in – the – bo-dy – but – made – a-live – by – the – Spir-it.*

Say it like this over and over again until you feel that you really know it.

So, how much do you want to grow in your Christian life?

Jesus said, "Blessed are those who hunger and thirst for righteousness." He went on to add this promise, "'for they will be filled.'" *Matthew 5:6*

Memorizing Scripture will help you become a stronger Christian if you are prayerful about it. So the first thing to do when you feel like giving up is to pray to God about how you feel.

Have you thought of memorizing Scripture with a friend?

If you think that would help, find a friend to work with you in memorizing Scripture.

It is also a good idea to ask at least one other Christian to pray for you as you set out to memorize Scripture.

Week 10: Review, review, review

No new verses
This week there are no new verses to learn. There are no verses to review. It's a time to reflect on how you are progressing.

Examination time
If you want to see how well you are doing, give yourself this simple test.

Write out all your verses for weeks 1–8 at one sitting. You should include the Bible references. Don't worry if you cannot remember all the topics. But write them down as you come to each verse, even if you have to look them up.

Then check each verse and reference carefully. Don't worry about any mistakes you may have made. Just relearn the verse.

Do this once on Monday and each day of the week until you know it perfectly, word for word.

"Pray in" a verse a day
Once you have managed to write out all your verses with 100% accuracy, select one verse a day from those you have learned and spend a little time "praying in" its message so that your heart is warmed by what it says.

You may say that you already spent time "praying in" each verse when you first learned it. But you may be surprised at how many new layers of meaning God unfolds in each verse as you learn more about yourself and about God.

> "'Were not our hearts burning within us while [Jesus] talked with us on the road and opened the Scriptures to us?'"
> *Luke 24:32*

When to review
In addition to the set times when you review your verses, think about how you can review them at other times. If you carry your Bible memory verse cards with you in your pocket, wallet, or purse, you may find some spare time in the day when you can review them.

Seven years' worth of waiting in lines

Someone has figured out that most of us spend up to seven years of our lives waiting in lines. These may be ideal moments for you to review your verses.

Go over in your mind one set of verses from one of the themes. Go through all the verses at one time. Then hold one verse at a time in your mind and meditate on it. See what it is saying at that moment.

Awake at night

If you wake up in the night, focus on one of your most recently learned verses and repeat it, "feeding" on its spiritual content.

> "I will praise the LORD who counsels me; even at night my heart instructs me." *Psalm 16:7*

Weeks 11–15: The Holy Spirit at work

THE HOLY SPIRIT	1/11/1

Helping you understand

We have not received the spirit of the world but the Spirit who is from God, that we may understand what God has freely given us.
1 Corinthians 2:12

THE HOLY SPIRIT	1/11/2

Fellowship

May the grace of the Lord Jesus Christ, and the love of God, and the fellowship of the Holy Spirit be with you all.
2 Corinthians 13:14

THE HOLY SPIRIT	1/12/1

Lives in you

Don't you know that you yourselves are God's temple and that God's Spirit lives in you?
1 Corinthians 3:16

THE HOLY SPIRIT	1/12/2

Brings joy

For the kingdom of God is not a matter of eating and drinking, but of righteousness, peace and joy in the Holy Spirit.
Romans 14:17

There are ten verses to learn under this new theme *The Holy Spirit at work.*

1 Corinthians 2:12	Helping you understand
2 Corinthians 13:14	Fellowship
1 Corinthians 3:16	Lives in you
Romans 14:17	Brings joy
Galatians 5:25	Keep in step with
Romans 8:26	Helps in prayer
1 John 4:13	God's gift
John 14:16	With you forever
Ephesians 5:18	Be filled
John 14:26	Teaches you

Remembering the topics

As with all the other verses, each of these ten verses about the Holy Spirit has been given a topic.

When reviewing verses, many people find it helpful to have a way of remembering which order they come in. For these verses a simple acrostic on the words HOLY SPIRIT has been devised. If you find it helpful, it is easy to use.

THE HOLY SPIRIT 1/13/1
Keep in step with

Since we live by the Spirit, let us keep in step with the Spirit.
Galatians 5:25

THE HOLY SPIRIT 1/13/2
Helps in prayer

In the same way, the Spirit helps us in our weakness. We do not know what we ought to pray for, but the Spirit himself intercedes for us with groans that words cannot express.
Romans 8:26

THE HOLY SPIRIT 1/14/1
God's gift

We know that we live in him and he in us, because he has given us of his Spirit.
1 John 4:13

THE HOLY SPIRIT 1/14/2
With you for ever

"And I will ask the Father, and he will give you another Counselor to be with you forever."
John 14:16

THE HOLY SPIRIT 1/15/1
Be filled

Do not get drunk on wine, which leads to debauchery. Instead, be filled with the Spirit.
Ephesians 5:18

THE HOLY SPIRIT 1/15/2
Teaches you

"But the Counselor, the Holy Spirit, whom the Father will send in my name, will teach you all things and will remind you of everything I have said to you."
John 14:26

All you have to do is to go through the letters making up the word HOLY SPIRIT trying to remember the word or words which relate to each letter.

HOLY SPIRIT acrostic

Helping you understand
Fell**O**wship
Lives in you
Brings jo**Y**
Keep in **S**tep with
Helps in **P**rayer
God's g**I**ft
With you foreve**R**
Be f**I**lled
Teaches you

More handy hints

We remember what we understand

If you don't understand any of the verses you are learning, look them up in a Bible commentary or ask somebody to explain them to you.

> "But the one who received the seed that fell on good soil is the man who hears the word and understands it. He produces a crop, yielding a hundred, sixty or thirty times what was sown."
> *Matthew 13:23*

Your mind accepts and remembers what it understands but tends to put up a barrier against remembering what it is unable to grasp or comprehend.

We focus on what we think is relevant

When people go shopping, even just window-shopping, they only take time to stop and look at what they are interested in.

If you believe that these Bible verses can transform your life, and if you strongly desire to be a more faithful disciple of Jesus, you will not need anyone to point out the value of memorizing Scripture. You will never stop wanting to absorb into your life more and more of God's Word.

How Scripture memory is relevant to you

Memorizing Scripture helps you to:

- **overcome worry.**

  "Great peace have they who love your law, and nothing can make them stumble."
  Psalm 119:165

- **defeat sin.**

  The Psalmist wrote:

  "I have hidden your word in my heart that I might not sin against you." *Psalm 119:11*

  "In your battle against Satan and sin you now have God's word tucked in your heart. Paul calls it "the sword of the Spirit, which is the word of God."
  Ephesians 6:17

Slow and steady wins the race

A whole number of things memorized at great speed are less likely to be remembered than a few things learned slowly.

Who can climb a pyramid?

According to an eastern proverb, there are only two creatures that can surmount the pyramids: the eagle and the snail.

Perseverance is a great Christian virtue and it is hard to overvalue its importance in memory work.

"'You have persevered and have endured hardships for my name, and have not grown weary.'" *Revelation 2:3*

Weeks 16–21: Bible promises

BIBLE PROMISES 1/16/1 Answered prayer "Again, I tell you that if two of you on earth agree about anything you ask for, it will be done for you by my Father in heaven." Matthew 18:19	**BIBLE PROMISES** 1/16/2 Burdened people "Come to me, all you who are weary and burdened, and I will give you rest." Matthew 11:28	**BIBLE PROMISES** 1/17/1 Christ's peace "Peace I leave with you; my peace I give you. I do not give to you as the world gives. Do not let your hearts be troubled and do not be afraid." John 14:27
BIBLE PROMISES 1/17/2 Death is not the end By his power God raised the Lord from the dead, and he will raise us also. 1 Corinthians 6:14	**BIBLE PROMISES** 1/18/1 Everlasting covenant ". . . I will make an everlasting covenant with them: I will never stop doing good to them, and I will inspire them to fear me, so that they will never turn away from me." Jeremiah 32:40	**BIBLE PROMISES** 1/18/2 Forgiveness As far as the east is from the west, so far has he removed our transgressions from us. Psalm 103:12

This theme about Bible promises is the longest so far and has twelve verses in it.

Promise boxes

In Victorian times some Christians would pass around a promise box on Sunday afternoons. It looked a little like a box of chocolates. Instead of chocolates it was filled with tiny scrolls with a promise from the Bible written on each scroll. People passed around the promise box and everyone took a scroll and treated it as their promise from God for the week.

A promise box has been used as a way to help you remember the twelve verses in this theme, each of which starts with a consecutive letter of the alphabet.

BIBLE PROMISES 1/19/1

God's presence

"Have I not commanded you? Be strong and courageous. Do not be terrified; do not be discouraged, for the LORD your God will be with you wherever you go."
Joshua 1:9

BIBLE PROMISES 1/19/2

Heart and spirit

"I will give you a new heart and put a new spirit in you; I will remove from you your heart of stone and give you a heart of flesh."
Ezekiel 36:26

BIBLE PROMISES 1/20/1

Instruction

I will instruct you and teach you in the way you should go; I will counsel you and watch over you.
Psalm 32:8

BIBLE PROMISES 1/20/2

Jesus' resurrection

. . . because he was teaching his disciples. He said to them, "The Son of Man is going to be betrayed into the hands of men. They will kill him, and after three days he will rise."
Mark 9:31

BIBLE PROMISES 1/21/1

Knowledge of God

His divine power has given us everything we need for life and godliness through our knowledge of him who called us by his own glory and goodness.
2 Peter 1:3

BIBLE PROMISES 1/21/2

Life from the Spirit

"The Spirit gives life; the flesh counts for nothing. The words I have spoken to you are spirit and they are life."
John 6:63

39

A–B–C–D–E–F–G–H–I–J–K–L

How to turn memorizing verses into Bible studies

Look at the context

Look up a verse in your Bible you have memorized and read the verses that surround it.

Use, for example, the last verse you have learned: Life from the Spirit. "'The Spirit gives life; the flesh counts for nothing. The words I have spoken to you are spirit and they are life.'"
John 6:63

Start by reading the paragraph in which the verse occurs, that is, John 6:61-65. Then look at the section from which the paragraph comes. The heading to the section given by *The New International Version* is "Many Disciples Desert Jesus." So John 6:63 is given by Jesus as an antidote to disciples who were grumbling and saying of Jesus' words, "'This is a hard teaching,'" *(John 6:60)*.

When you understand this background to the verse, you can see why Jesus said these words and appreciate just how important they are.

Ask questions about the verse

Is there a command, a promise, or a warning – or all three – in the verse?

Link up verses

The following list has all one hundred Bible verses used in this course. The verses are followed by the number of the week in which they appear.

Start by reading the chapters in the Bible where a number of Bible verses are used in different weeks. There are five verses from John chapter 14, for example, where each verse comes in a different week. Read all of John chapter 14, and then see how the four verses in the different weeks are used.

Joshua		Mark		Romans		2 Corinthians		1 Peter	
1:9	19	9:31	20	3:23	4	1:3	41	2:24	6
				5:1	23	5:14	27	3:15	40
Psalm		John		5:5	2	5:17	30	3:18	5
23:1	43	3:16	1	5:8	26	13:14	11	5:7	41
23:2	43	5:24	31	6:23	5				
23:3	44	6:35	7	8:1	31	Galatians		2 Peter	
23:4	44	6:37	32	8:26	13	2:20	28	1:3	21
23:5	45	6:63	21	8:39	3	5:25	13		
23:6	45	8:12	7	12:1	33			1 John	
27:5	42	10:9	8	14:17	12	Ephesians		1:9	24
32:8	20	10:11	8			1:7	24	2:2	29
103:12	18	10:29	32	1 Corinthians		2:14	22	3:18	33
119:9	36	11:25	9	2:12	11	2:16	23	4:10	26
		14:6	9	3:16	12	5:2	27	4:13	14
Isaiah		14:16	14	6:14	17	5:3	36	4:16	3
41:10	35	14:21	35	12:31	46	5:18	15	5:13	30
53:6	4	14:26	15	13:1	46				
		14:27	17	13:2	47	Colossians		Revelation	
Jeremiah		15:7	34	13:3	47	1:20	22	3:20	6
32:40	18	15:9	1	13:4	48	21:4	42		
		15:13	2	13:5	48				
Ezekiel				13:6	49	Hebrews			
36:26	19	Acts		13:7	49	9:26	28		
		5:31	25	13:8	50	10:14	29		
Matthew		10:43	25	13:9	50	11:6	37		
4:19	39			13:10	51				
5:16	39			13:11	51	James			
11:28	16			13:12	52	4:7	37		
18:19	16			13:13	52				
18:20	34								
28:19	40								

Weeks 22–29: Jesus and his cross

JESUS AND HIS CROSS 1/22/1
Peace through Christ's death

And through him to reconcile to himself all things, whether things on earth or things in heaven, by making peace through his blood, shed on the cross.
Colossians 1:20

JESUS AND HIS CROSS 1/22/2
Jesus is our peace

For he himself is our peace, who has made the two one and has destroyed the barrier, the dividing wall of hostility.
Ephesians 2:14

JESUS AND HIS CROSS 1/23/1
Peace in place of hostility

. . . and in this one body to reconcile both of them to God through the cross, by which he put to death their hostility.
Ephesians 2:16

JESUS AND HIS CROSS 1/23/2
Peace with God

Therefore, since we have been justified through faith, we have peace with God through our Lord Jesus Christ.
Romans 5:1

JESUS AND HIS CROSS 1/24/1
Forgiveness and cleansing

If we confess our sins, he is faithful and just and will forgive us our sins and purify us from all unrighteousness.
1 John 1:9

JESUS AND HIS CROSS 1/24/2
Forgiveness and redemption

In him we have redemption through his blood, the forgiveness of sins, in accordance with the riches of God's grace.
Ephesians 1:7

JESUS AND HIS CROSS 1/25/1
Forgiveness and belief

"All the prophets testify about him that everyone who believes in him receives forgiveness of sins through his name."
Acts 10:43

JESUS AND HIS CROSS 1/25/2
Forgiveness and repentance

"God exalted him to his own right hand as Prince and Savior that he might give repentance and forgiveness of sins to Israel."
Acts 5:31

JESUS AND HIS CROSS 1/26/1
Love for sinners

But God demonstrates his own love for us in this: While we were still sinners, Christ died for us.
Romans 5:8

JESUS AND HIS CROSS 1/26/2
Love and expiation
for sins

This is love: not that
we loved God, but that
he loved us and sent
his Son as an atoning
sacrifice for our
sins.
1 John 4:10

JESUS AND HIS CROSS 1/27/1
Compelled by Christ's
love

For Christ's love
compels us, because
we are convinced that
one died for all, and
therefore all died.
2 Corinthians 5:14

JESUS AND HIS CROSS 1/27/2
Love and Jesus giving
himself

. . . and live a life of
love, just as Christ
loved us and gave
himself up for us as
a fragrant offering
and sacrifice to God.
Ephesians 5:2

JESUS AND HIS CROSS 1/28/1
Sacrifice and love

I have been crucified
with Christ and I no
longer live, but
Christ lives in me.
The life I live in the
body, I live by faith in
the Son of God, who
lived me and gave
himself for me.
Galatians 2:20

JESUS AND HIS CROSS 1/28/2
The sacrifice of
Jesus himself
Then Christ would have
had to suffer many
times since the
creation of the world.
But now he has
appeared once for all at
the end of the ages to
do away with sin by the
sacrifice of himself.
Hebrews 9:26

JESUS AND HIS CROSS 1/29/1
Jesus' one sacrifice

. . . because by one
sacrifice he has made
perfect for ever
those who are being
made holy.
Hebrews 10:14

JESUS AND HIS CROSS 1/29/2
Sacrifice for our
sins

He is the atoning
sacrifice for our
sins, and not only for
ours but also for the
sins of the whole
world.
1 John 2:2

Visualizing

One way of picturing these sixteen verses
about Jesus and his cross is to divide
them into four and link each set of four
to the four points of the cross. Label
these points, WIDTH, LENGTH,
HEIGHT, and DEPTH, following
Paul's verse about the love of Jesus: ". . .
to grasp how wide and long and high and
deep is the love of Christ . . ."
Ephesians 3:18

"I'm slipping. What do I do now?"

Don't give up!

There may be overwhelming personal reasons, like illness or problems at home or work, that have made it impossible for you to stay on track.

Don't worry if you have been forced to stop. Give it a break and return to it later on.

The sin problem

This may not be the reason why you stopped, but it does stop some people. It's been said that "The Bible will keep you from sin or sin will keep you from the Bible." Some people stop memorizing Scripture because one sin, or a number of sins, have overwhelmed their lives.

It may seem like the end of the world, or at least the end of your Christian life, but it need not be. It looked like the end for King David when he committed adultery with Bathsheba and arranged for her husband Uriah to be killed in battle. But God restored David.

The remedy

Read passages like 1 John 1:5-10, confess your sin, make right with God whatever needs to be made right, and carry on in your Christian life.

"This is the message we have heard from him and declare to you: God is light; in him there is no darkness at all. If we claim to have fellowship with him yet walk in the darkness, we lie and do not live by the truth. But if we walk in the light, as he is in the light, we have fellowship with one another, and the blood of Jesus, his Son, purifies us from all sin. If we claim to be without sin, we deceive ourselves and the truth is not in us. If we confess our sins, he is faithful and just and will forgive us our sins and purify us from all unrighteousness. If we claim we have not sinned, we make him out to be a liar and his word has no place in our lives."
1 John 1:5-10

Remember some of the reasons for memorizing Scripture

God's word in our hearts keeps our feet from slipping.	*Read Psalm 37:28-31*
It drives Satan away when he is tempting us, as Jesus knew.	*Read Matthew 4:1-11*
Knowing the word of God was, for the psalmist, a key to purity.	*Read Psalm 119:9-11*
The word is the sword to defeat the devil's plots to bring us down.	*Read Ephesians 6:13-18*

I feel bored

Ask God to restore the joy of your salvation.

"Restore to me the joy of your salvation." *Psalm 51:12*

No Christian escapes the need for forgiveness

"If you, O LORD, kept a record of sins, O LORD, who could stand? But with you there is forgiveness; therefore you are feared." *Psalm 130:3-4*

Weeks 30–32: "How can I be sure that I am a Christian?"

HOW CAN I BE SURE? 1/30/1 From death to life Therefore, if anyone is in Christ he is a new creation; the old has gone, the new has come! 2 Corinthians 5:17	**HOW CAN I BE SURE? 1/30/2** Eternal life I write these things to you who believe in the name of the Son of God so that you may know that you have eternal life. 1 John 5:13	**HOW CAN I BE SURE? 1/31/1** Promised "I tell you the truth, whoever hears my word and believes him who sent me has eternal life and will not be condemned; he has crossed over from death to life." John 5:24
HOW CAN I BE SURE? 1/31/2 God's call Therefore, there is now no condemnation for those who are in Christ Jesus. Romans 8:1	**HOW CAN I BE SURE? 1/32/1** Welcomed "All the Father gives me will come to me, and whoever comes to me I will never drive away." John 6:37	**HOW CAN I BE SURE? 1/32/2** Safe "My Father, who has given them to me, is greater than all; no one can snatch them out of my Father's hand." John 10:29

One of the most debilitating things that can happen to Christians is when they think that they may not be Christians after all. They may entertain grave doubts that Jesus ever came into the their lives or whether he is still with them.

These six arrows are ideal for shooting at the target of doubt, as they will each score a bull's-eye.

Weeks 33–37: "How can I grow as a Christian?"

HOW CAN I GROW? 1/33/1
Dedication

Therefore, I urge you, brothers, in view of God's mercy, to offer your bodies as living sacrifices, holy and pleasing to God – this is your spiritual act of worship.
Romans 12:1

HOW CAN I GROW? 1/33/2
Action

Dear children, let us not love with words or tongue but with actions and in truth.
1 John 3:18

HOW CAN I GROW? 1/34/1
With others

"For where two or three come together in my name, there am I with them."
Matthew 18:20

HOW CAN I GROW? 1/34/2
Pray

"If you remain in me and my words remain in you, ask whatever you wish, and it will be given you."
John 15:7

HOW CAN I GROW? 1/35/1
Obey

"Whoever has my commands and obeys them, he is the one who loves me. He who loves me will be loved by my Father, and I too will love him and show myself to him."
John 14:21

HOW CAN I GROW? 1/35/2
Strength

"So do not fear, for I am with you; do not be dismayed, for I am your God. I will strengthen you and help you; I will uphold you with my righteous right hand."
Isaiah 41:10

Birth – growth

Birth should lead to growth in our physical lives. It is exactly the same in our spiritual lives. Peter speaks to us about growth in this verse where the word milk stands for God's Word.

"Like newborn babies, crave pure spiritual milk, so that by it you may grow up in your salvation, now that you have tasted that the Lord is good." 1 Peter 2:2-3

HOW CAN I GROW? 1/36/1
Purity

But among you there must be not even a hint of sexual immorality, or of any kind of impurity, or of greed, because these are improper for God's holy people.
Ephesians 5:3

HOW CAN I GROW? 1/36/2
Bible

How can a young man keep his way pure? By living according to your word.
Psalm 119:9

HOW CAN I GROW? 1/37/1
Resist

Submit yourselves, then, to God. Resist the devil, and he will flee from you.
James 4:7

HOW CAN I GROW? 1/37/2
Faith

And without faith it is impossible to please God, because anyone who comes to him must believe that he exists and that he rewards those who earnestly seek him.
Hebrews 11:6

Week 38: Review, review, review

Learning a verse

It has been said that a Bible verse is not really memorized until you have reviewed it ____ times. How many times do you think it is necessary to review a verse before you are certain that you will never forget it? Six times, twenty-six times, eighty-six times? Well, the answer many writers on this topic give is *one hundred* times.

So, you should never think of reviewing as a waste of time. Every time you review a verse, you are helping your memory.

I can't keep up

It really does not matter how many verses you learn in a year. What matters is that the verses that you do learn make an impact on your spiritual growth. So, if you prefer to learn one verse a week, that's fine. Just adapt this course to suit what suits you best.

A good tip is not to learn more verses until you have reviewed the ones you have already learned. You need to be totally confident that you know them with 100% accuracy. This may mean that you will need to spend an extra week reviewing. If that is necessary, fine.

As you sleep, as you wake up

Try reviewing your verses as you go to sleep at night.
- Start with the verse you have most recently learned.
- The next night try to review all the verses in the theme you are currently learning.
- The next night review the previous theme.
- The next night review the theme before that, and take one theme a night until you reach the first theme.
- The next night review two themes. Keep on doing this until you are able to review all your Bible verses at one time!
- Try the same thing as you wake up.

Build up to this very slowly. Take your time.

Day and night

"Blessed is the man who does not walk in the counsel of the wicked or stand in the way of sinners or sit in the seat of mockers. But his delight is in the law of the LORD, and on his law he meditates day and night. He is like a tree planted by streams of water, which yields its fruit in season and whose leaf does not wither. Whatever he does prospers." *Psalm 1:1-3*

More reasons for memorizing Scripture

Keep your goal in sight

One way to stop yourself from being deflected from a lifetime habit of memorizing Scripture is to keep focused on why you are doing this. It is much easier to learn something if you are totally convinced of its vital importance.

Psalm 119

This is the longest psalm and the longest chapter in the Bible. Nearly all of its 176 verses tell us something about God's Word. It is divided into twenty-two sections, one for each letter of the Hebrew alphabet.

Read one eight-verse section a day and find the seven different words the psalmist uses for God's Word.

The importance of knowing and following God's Word is provided here in great detail. It will stimulate you to keep moving ahead with your own memorization of Scripture.

Word, decrees, promises

- "Direct my footsteps according to your word; let no sin rule over me." Psalm 119:133
- "Make your face shine upon your servant and teach me your decrees." Psalm 119:135
- "My eyes stay open through the watches of the night, that I may meditate on your promises." Psalm 119:148

The encouragement of the Scriptures

The writers of the New Testament often said how much we can learn from the Old Testament.

"For everything that was written in the past was written to teach us, so that through endurance and the encouragement of the Scriptures we might have hope." Romans 15:4

Memorize for others

Asking God to build you up in your Christian life is never a selfish prayer. Others will always benefit.

By memorizing the Bible verses suggested for the next two weeks – on pages 54-55 "Witnessing for Jesus" – you will feel better equipped to talk about Jesus with other people.

"Ezra had devoted himself to the study . . ."

"For Ezra had devoted himself to the study and observance of the Law of the LORD, and to teaching its decrees and laws in Israel." *Ezra 7:10*

"Do your best . . ."

"Do your best to present yourself to God as one approved, a workman who does not need to be ashamed and who correctly handles the word of truth." *2 Timothy 2:15*

Weeks 39–40: Witnessing for Jesus

WITNESSING FOR JESUS
1/39/1
Fishing for Jesus

"Come, follow me," Jesus said, "and I will make you fishers of men."
Matthew 4:19

WITNESSING FOR JESUS
1/39/2
Shine

"In the same way, let your light shine before men, that they may see your good deeds and praise your Father in heaven."
Matthew 5:16

WITNESSING FOR JESUS
1/40/1
Give a reason
But in your hearts set apart Christ as Lord. Always be prepared to give an answer to everyone who asks you to give the reason for the hope that you have. But do this with gentleness and respect. 1 Peter 3:15

WITNESSING FOR JESUS
1/40/2
Make disciples

"Therefore go and make disciples of all nations, baptizing them in the name of the Father and of the Son and of the Holy Spirit."
Matthew 28:19

The pull-down chart

The pull-down chart at the end of the book suggests that a way to remember the theme "Witnessing for Jesus" is the symbol of a fishing rod depicted by a scene of fish being caught.

Remembering the order

The four topics under this theme with their verses are:

Matthew 4:19	Fishing for Jesus
Matthew 5:16	Shine
1 Peter 3:15	Give a reason
Matthew 28:19	Make disciples

When it comes to reviewing verses, especially when you are doing this in your head and are not able to look at your memory cards, it is helpful to be able to remember the order in which the topics come for each theme.

On pages 34–35, the idea of an acrostic on the words HOLY SPIRIT was suggested for memorizing the order of the ten topics under the theme of the Holy Spirit

Do It Yourself

The best memory aids are the ones you make up yourself. So devise a way to remember the order of these four topics on the theme Witnessing for Jesus. Jot it down on the back of memory card 1/39/1 in case you forget it.

Weeks 41–42: Words of comfort

WORDS OF COMFORT 1/41/1
God of comfort

Praise be to the God and Father of our Lord Jesus Christ, the Father of compassion and the God of all comfort.
2 Corinthians 1:3

WORDS OF COMFORT 1/41/2
God cares

Cast all your anxiety on him because he cares for you.
1 Peter 5:7

WORDS OF COMFORT 1/42/2
Safety

For in the day of trouble he will keep me safe in his dwelling; he will hide me in the shelter of his tabernacle and set me high upon a rock.
Psalm 27:5

WORDS OF COMFORT 1/42/2
No crying

"He will wipe every tear from their eyes. There will be no more death or mourning or crying or pain, for the old order of things has passed away."
Revelation 21:4

Thermometer
On the pull-out chart a thermometer is the symbol used to remember the theme "Words of comfort."

Hospital bed
A hospital bed is suggested as the memory aid. There are four bottles at the bedside. These labeled bottles have the following names on them:
- God of comfort
- God cares
- Safety
- No crying

The ministry of comfort
All Christians can bring God's comfort to people every day.
   "Rejoice with those who rejoice; mourn with those who mourn." *Romans 12:15*

God
of
Comfort

How to learn longer passages of Scripture

1. Select your chapter
Once you've chosen a chapter, don't change it.

2. Familiarize yourself with the whole chapter
Read the chapter from start to finish many times – ten times would not be too many – before you start memorizing even the first verse.

3. Understand the chapter
You may want to read a commentary or two about the chapter to help you understand it.

4. Do a mini Bible study on the chapter
Write down the following things about it:
• its main theme
• its key word or words
• its main sections

5. Write the chapter out
Copy the whole chapter onto your Bible memory cards. Put one verse only on each card. Use the name of the Bible book and its chapter as the theme.

Don't worry about putting a topic on the cards as you write out the chapter. You can do this as you come to learn each verse. If you become completely stuck about what word or words to use for a topic, chose one from the verse itself.

Writing out verses

If you are learning poetry-style verses from the Psalms, it is usually helpful to follow the style that your Bible uses. But you may find that a passage like Romans 8:38-39 is easier to remember if you do not simply copy it out as run-on words, as printed in your Bible.

"For I am convinced that neither death nor life, neither angels nor demons, neither the present nor the future, nor any powers, neither height nor depth, nor anything else in all creation, will be able to separate us from the love of God that is in Christ Jesus our Lord."
Romans 8:38-39

Use your imagination

"For I am convinced that
neither death nor life,
neither angels nor demons,
neither the present nor the future,
nor any powers,
neither height nor depth,
nor anything else in all creation,
will be able to separate us
    from the love of God
        that is in Christ Jesus our Lord."
Romans 8:38-39

PSALM 23 1/43/1	PSALM 23 1/43/2	PSALM 23 1/44/1
Shepherd	Pasture	Restores
The LORD is my shepherd, I shall not be in want. Psalm 23:1	He makes me lie down in green pastures, he leads me beside quiet waters, Psalm 23:2	he restores my soul. He guides me in paths of righteousness for his name's sake. Psalm 23:3

PSALM 23 1/44/2	PSALM 23 1/45/1	PSALM 23 1/45/2
Comfort	Anointed	Forever
Even though I walk through the valley of the shadow of death, I will fear no evil, for you are with me; your rod and your staff, they comfort me. Psalm 23:4	You prepare a table before me in the presence of my enemies. You anoint my head with oil; my cup overflows. Psalm 23:5	Surely goodness and love will follow me all the days of my life, and I will dwell in the house of the LORD forever. . Psalm 23:6

Crook

In the pull-out chart a shepherd's crook is suggested as the symbol by which this theme is remembered.

Shepherd and sheep

The memory aid is "shepherd and sheep."

When you begin choosing your own symbols and memory aids for the themes you select for learning in year 2, there is nothing wrong with choosing obvious and straightforward ideas such as "shepherd and sheep." However, memory training experts suggest that we are more likely to remember things if we use ideas which are:

• moving
• funny – the more humorous the better
• memorable

Topics for Psalm 23

The topics for each verse for Psalm 23 are as follows:

Psalm 23:1	Shepherd
Psalm 23:2	Pasture
Psalm 23:3	Restores
Psalm 23:4	Comfort
Psalm 23:5	Anointed
Psalm 23:6	Forever

Remembering the topics

With such well-known verses and with consecutive verses, you may feel that you do not need any further help in remembering the topics.

But if you do, work out how you are going to remember the words "Shepherd, Pasture, Restores, Comfort, Anointed," and "Forever" in a memorable way. One way to remember key words is to picture them in an unusual setting – on the top of the Empire State Building, for example.

1 CORINTHIANS 12   1/46/1
Excellent way

But eagerly desire the greater gifts. And now I will show you the most excellent way.
1 Corinthians 12:31

1 CORINTHIANS 13   1/46/2
Tongues

If I speak in the tongues of men and of angels, but have not love, I am only a resounding gong or a clanging cymbal.
1 Corinthians 13:1

1 CORINTHIANS 13   1/47/1
Prophecy

If I have the gift of prophecy and can fathom all mysteries and all knowledge, and if I have a faith that can move mountains, but have not love, I am nothing.
1 Corinthians 13:2

1 CORINTHIANS 13   1/47/2
Giving

If I give all I possess to the poor and surrender my body to the flames, but have not love, I gain nothing.
1 Corinthians 13:3

1 CORINTHIANS 13   1/48/1
Patient

Love is patient, love is kind. It does not envy, it does not boast, it is not proud.
1 Corinthians 13:4

1 CORINTHIANS 13   1/48/2
Not rude

It is not rude, it is not self-seeking, it is not easily angered, it keeps no record of wrongs.
1 Corinthians 13:5

1 CORINTHIANS 13   1/49/1
Rejoices in truth

Love does not delight in evil but rejoices with the truth.
1 Corinthians 13:6

1 CORINTHIANS 13   1/49/2
Trusts

It always protects, always trusts, always hopes, always perseveres.
1 Corinthians 13:7

1 CORINTHIANS 13   1/50/1
Never fails

Love never fails. But where there are prophecies, they will cease; where there are tongues, they will be stilled; where there is knowledge, it will pass away.
1 Corinthians 13:8

Partial

For we know in part and we prophesy in part,
1 Corinthians 13:9

Perfection

but when perfection comes, the imperfect disappears.
1 Corinthians 13:10

Face to face

When I was a child, I talked like a child, I thought like a child, I reasoned like a child. When I became a man, I put childish ways behind me.
1 Corinthians 13:11

Childish ways

Now we see but a poor reflection as in a mirror; then we shall see face to face. Now I know in part; then I shall know fully, even as I am fully known.
1 Corinthians 13:12

The greatest

And now these three remain: faith, hope and love. But the greatest of these is love.
1 Corinthians 13:13

Heart symbol

In the pull-out chart you will see that a heart symbol has been used to remember 1 Corinthians 13. The idea comes from an old Beatles song which says "All you need is love; yeah, yeah, yeah."

63

Topics

The topics for remembering the theme of 1 Corinthians are:

1 Corinthians

12:31	Excellent way	13:7	Trusts
13:1	Tongues	13:8	Never fails
13:2	Prophecy	13:9	Partial
13:3	Giving	13:10	Perfection
13:4	Patient	13:11	Face to face
13:5	Not rude	13:12	Childish ways
13:6	Rejoices in truth	13:13	The greatest

You may want to devise a catchy way to remember the order of these fourteen verses.

How to make your plan for next year

1. Make your own collection
As you read through the Bible this year, jot down any Bible verses that strike you as being ideal verses to remember. Keep a piece of paper in your Bible for this purpose. Then arrange them into themes. You just need one hundred to be all set for next year.

2. Memorize chapters
If you want to remember sections of the Bible, then the following chapters and parts of chapters would be suitable ones.
• Isaiah 52:13–53:12
• John 15:1-27
• Romans 8:1-39
• Philippians 2:1-18
These four passages make up one hundred verses.

3. Review plan
Work out your own review plan. Base it on the review plan for the year on pages 16-17, "How do I review verses?"

4. Memory helps
Provide memory helps for each theme as you go along. Try to work out an overall plan so your themes fit into the fifty-two weeks of the year.